This Logbook Belongs To:

Gracie the herPatoligist

Sample Log

Name: __Black Racer snake__

Scientific Name: __Coluber constrictor__

Date: __June 14, 2019__   Time: __2 pm__

Location: __Backyard bushes and grass (Florida)__

Season

Winter   Spring

(Summer)   Fall

Weather

Temperature: __87° F__

Habitat

Bushes and grass in hot climate.

Physical Description

Colors: __Black__   Size: __Medium sized, 2 feet long__

Markings: __Solid black no markings__

Behavior

Slithered away as soon as it saw me. Hid in the bushes. Looked scared. I saw it stick out its tongue a few times.

Sketch

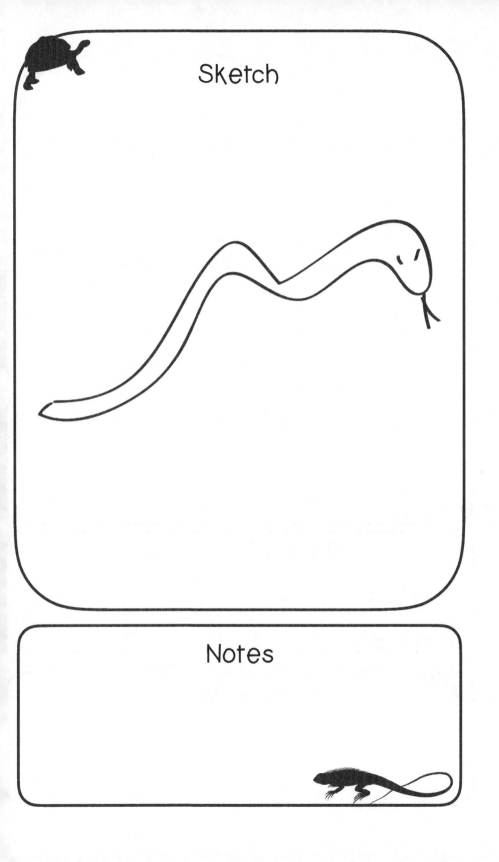

Notes

Name: horned lizard

Scientific Name: _____

Date: June 1st 2023   Time: 5:30 Pm

Location: Iron Mountain

Season

Winter   Spring

(Summer) Fall

Weather

Temperature: 80

Habitat

Dry arid desert habitat

Physical Description

Colors: Baish Brown   Size: 10 inches

Markings: Baish brown and black Patern

Behavior

Calm trying to camoflosh

Sketch

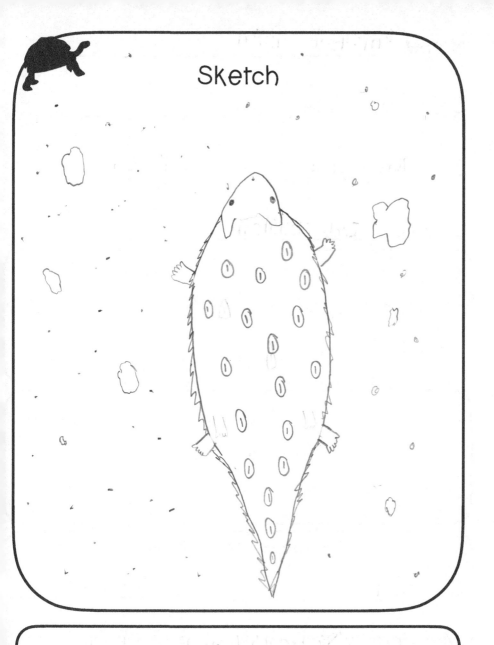

Notes

Suprisisingly calm, trying to hide or camoflosh

Name: Bluebelly lizard

Scientific Name: _____

Date: November 4th 2023   Time: 11:25 am

Location: Iron mountain

Season
Winter   Spring

Summer   (Fall)

Weather

Temperature: 82

Habitat
Dry arid landscape

Physical Description
Colors: Dark brown brown boish   Size: 3-4 inches

Markings: typical, dark brown light Brown down spi

Behavior
Skidish because out
in open busy trail

Sketch

Notes

Very Small fun fact there
was two

Name: Bearded dragon

Scientific Name: _____

Date: Augest 16th 2023   Time: 8:00

Location: _____

Season

Winter   Spring

Summer   (Fall)

Weather

Temperature: 48

Habitat
Exoltara large

Physical Description

Colors: BaiSh   Size: 25 inches

Markings: tYPichal

Behavior
Calm lazy like a
couch Potato

Sketch

LiZZY

Notes

I wish lizzy would Move
PS it's My Class Pet.

Name: _____

Scientific Name: _____

Date:_____   Time:_____

Location: _____

Season	Weather
Winter Spring Summer Fall	Temperature: _____

Habitat

Physical Description

Colors: _____   Size: _____

Markings:_____

Behavior

Sketch

Notes

Name: _____

Scientific Name: _____

Date: _____   Time: _____

Location: _____

Season	Weather
Winter Spring	
Summer Fall	Temperature: _____

Habitat

Physical Description

Colors: _____   Size: _____

Markings: _____

Behavior

Sketch

Notes

Name: _____

Scientific Name: _____

Date:_____   Time:_____

Location: _____

Season	Weather
Winter Spring Summer Fall	 Temperature: _____

Habitat

Physical Description

Colors: _____   Size: _____

Markings:_____

Behavior

Sketch

Notes

Name: _____

Scientific Name: _____

Date:_____   Time:_____

Location: _____

Season	Weather
Winter Spring Summer Fall	 Temperature: ____

Habitat

Physical Description

Colors: _____   Size: _____

Markings:_____

Behavior

Sketch

Notes

Name: _____

Scientific Name: _____

Date: _____   Time: _____

Location: _____

Season

Winter   Spring

Summer   Fall

Weather

Temperature: _____

Habitat

Physical Description

Colors: _____   Size: _____

Markings: _____

Behavior

Sketch

Notes

Name: _____

Scientific Name: _____

Date: _____   Time: _____

Location: _____

Season	Weather
Winter Spring Summer Fall	 Temperature: _____

Habitat

Physical Description

Colors: _____   Size: _____

Markings: _____

Behavior

Sketch

Notes

Name: _____

Scientific Name: _____

Date: _____   Time: _____

Location: _____

<table>
<tr><td>

Season

Winter   Spring

Summer   Fall

</td><td>

Weather

Temperature: _____

</td></tr>
</table>

Habitat

Physical Description

Colors: _____   Size: _____

Markings: _____

Behavior

Sketch

Notes

Name: _____

Scientific Name: _____

Date: _____   Time: _____

Location: _____

Season	Weather
Winter Spring	☀ ☁ ☁ ☁ 💨
Summer Fall	Temperature: _____

Habitat

Physical Description

Colors: _____   Size: _____

Markings: _____

Behavior

Sketch

Notes

Name: _____

Scientific Name: _____

Date: _____   Time: _____

Location: _____

Season	Weather
Winter Spring	☀ ☁ 🌧 🌨 💨
Summer Fall	Temperature: ____

Habitat

Physical Description

Colors: _____   Size: _____

Markings: _____

Behavior

Sketch

Notes

Name: _____

Scientific Name: _____

Date:_____   Time:_____

Location: _____

Season	Weather
Winter Spring	
Summer Fall	Temperature: _____

Habitat

Physical Description

Colors: _____   Size: _____

Markings:_____

Behavior

Sketch

Notes

Name: _____

Scientific Name: _____

Date: _____   Time: _____

Location: _____

Season	Weather
Winter Spring Summer Fall	☀ ☁ 🌧 🌨 💨 Temperature: ____

Habitat

Physical Description

Colors: _____   Size: _____

Markings: _____

Behavior

Sketch

Notes

Name: _____

Scientific Name: _____

Date: _____   Time: _____

Location: _____

Season

Winter   Spring

Summer   Fall

Weather

Temperature: _____

Habitat

Physical Description

Colors: _____   Size: _____

Markings: _____

Behavior

Sketch

Notes

Name: _____

Scientific Name: _____

Date:_____   Time:_____

Location: _____

Season

Winter   Spring

Summer   Fall

Weather

Temperature: _____

Habitat

Physical Description

Colors: _____   Size: _____

Markings:_____

Behavior

Sketch

Notes

Name: _____

Scientific Name: _____

Date: _____   Time: _____

Location: _____

Season	Weather
Winter Spring	☀ ☁ ☔ ❄ 🌬
Summer Fall	Temperature: _____

Habitat

Physical Description

Colors: _____   Size: _____

Markings: _____

Behavior

Sketch

Notes

Name: _____

Scientific Name: _____

Date: _____   Time: _____

Location: _____

Season

Winter   Spring

Summer   Fall

Weather

Temperature: _____

Habitat

Physical Description

Colors: _____   Size: _____

Markings: _____

Behavior

Sketch

Notes

Name: _____

Scientific Name: _____

Date: _____   Time: _____

Location: _____

Season	Weather
Winter Spring	
Summer Fall	Temperature: _____

Habitat

Physical Description

Colors: _____   Size: _____

Markings: _____

Behavior

Sketch

Notes

Name: _____

Scientific Name: _____

Date: _____   Time: _____

Location: _____

Season	Weather
Winter Spring	
Summer Fall	Temperature: _____

Habitat

Physical Description

Colors: _____   Size: _____

Markings: _____

Behavior

Sketch

Notes

Name: _____

Scientific Name: _____

Date:_____   Time:_____

Location: _____

Season	Weather
Winter Spring	
Summer Fall	Temperature: _____

Habitat

Physical Description

Colors: _____   Size: _____

Markings:_____

Behavior

Sketch

Notes

Name: _____

Scientific Name: _____

Date: _____   Time: _____

Location: _____

Season	Weather
Winter Spring	
Summer Fall	Temperature: _____

Habitat

Physical Description

Colors: _____   Size: _____

Markings: _____

Behavior

Sketch

Notes

Name: _____

Scientific Name: _____

Date: _____   Time: _____

Location: _____

Season	Weather
Winter Spring	
Summer Fall	Temperature: _____

Habitat

Physical Description

Colors: _____   Size: _____

Markings: _____

Behavior

Sketch

Notes

Name: _____

Scientific Name: _____

Date: _____   Time: _____

Location: _____

Season

Winter   Spring

Summer   Fall

Weather

Temperature: _____

Habitat

Physical Description

Colors: _____   Size: _____

Markings: _____

Behavior

Sketch

Notes

Name: _____

Scientific Name: _____

Date:_____   Time:_____

Location: _____

Season	Weather
Winter Spring	
Summer Fall	Temperature: _____

Habitat

Physical Description

Colors: _____   Size: _____

Markings:_____

Behavior

Sketch

Notes

Name: _____

Scientific Name: _____

Date: _____   Time: _____

Location: _____

Season

Winter   Spring

Summer   Fall

Weather

Temperature: _____

Habitat

Physical Description

Colors: _____   Size: _____

Markings: _____

Behavior

Sketch

Notes

Name: _____

Scientific Name: _____

Date: _____   Time: _____

Location: _____

Season

Winter   Spring

Summer   Fall

Weather

Temperature: _____

Habitat

Physical Description

Colors: _____   Size: _____

Markings: _____

Behavior

Sketch

Notes

Name: _____

Scientific Name: _____

Date: _____ Time: _____

Location: _____

Season

Winter   Spring

Summer   Fall

Weather

Temperature: _____

Habitat

Physical Description

Colors: _____ Size: _____

Markings: _____

Behavior

Sketch

Notes

Name: _____

Scientific Name: _____

Date: _____   Time: _____

Location: _____

Season	Weather
Winter Spring	
Summer Fall	Temperature: _____

Habitat

Physical Description

Colors: _____   Size: _____

Markings: _____

Behavior

Sketch

Notes

Name: _____

Scientific Name: _____

Date:_____   Time:_____

Location: _____

Season	Weather
Winter Spring	
Summer Fall	Temperature: _____

Habitat

Physical Description

Colors: _____   Size: _____

Markings:_____

Behavior

Sketch

Notes

Name: _____

Scientific Name: _____

Date:_____   Time:_____

Location: _____

Season	Weather
Winter Spring	
Summer Fall	Temperature: ____

Habitat

Physical Description

Colors: _____ Size: _____

Markings:_____

Behavior

Sketch

Notes

Name: _____

Scientific Name: _____

Date:_____   Time:_____

Location: _____

Season	Weather
Winter Spring	
Summer Fall	Temperature: _____

Habitat

Physical Description

Colors: _____   Size: _____

Markings:_____

Behavior

Sketch

Notes

Name: _____

Scientific Name: _____

Date: _____   Time: _____

Location: _____

Season

Winter   Spring

Summer   Fall

Weather

Temperature: _____

Habitat

Physical Description

Colors: _____   Size: _____

Markings: _____

Behavior

Sketch

Notes

Name: _____

Scientific Name: _____

Date: _____   Time: _____

Location: _____

Season	Weather
Winter Spring	
Summer Fall	Temperature: _____

Habitat

Physical Description

Colors: _____   Size: _____

Markings: _____

Behavior

Sketch

Notes

Name: _____

Scientific Name: _____

Date: _____   Time: _____

Location: _____

Season	Weather
Winter Spring	
Summer Fall	Temperature: _____

Habitat

Physical Description

Colors: _____   Size: _____

Markings: _____

Behavior

Sketch

Notes

Name: _____

Scientific Name: _____

Date: _____   Time: _____

Location: _____

Season

Winter   Spring

Summer   Fall

Weather

Temperature: _____

Habitat

Physical Description

Colors: _____   Size: _____

Markings: _____

Behavior

Sketch

Notes

Name: _____

Scientific Name: _____

Date: _____   Time: _____

Location: _____

<table>
<tr><td>

Season

Winter   Spring

Summer   Fall

</td><td>

Weather

☀ ☁ 🌧 🌨 💨

Temperature: _____

</td></tr>
</table>

Habitat

Physical Description

Colors: _____   Size: _____

Markings: _____

Behavior

Sketch

Notes

Name: _____

Scientific Name: _____

Date: _____   Time: _____

Location: _____

<table>
<tr><th>Season</th><th>Weather</th></tr>
</table>

Season

Winter   Spring

Summer   Fall

Weather

Temperature: _____

Habitat

Physical Description

Colors: _____   Size: _____

Markings: _____

Behavior

Sketch

Notes

Name: _____

Scientific Name: _____

Date: _____   Time: _____

Location: _____

Season

Winter   Spring

Summer   Fall

Weather

Temperature: _____

Habitat

Physical Description

Colors: _____   Size: _____

Markings: _____

Behavior

Sketch

Notes

Name: _____

Scientific Name: _____

Date: _____   Time: _____

Location: _____

Season	Weather
Winter Spring	
Summer Fall	Temperature: _____

Habitat

Physical Description

Colors: _____ Size: _____

Markings: _____

Behavior

Sketch

Notes

Name: _____

Scientific Name: _____

Date: _____   Time: _____

Location: _____

Season	Weather
Winter Spring	
Summer Fall	Temperature: _____

Habitat

Physical Description

Colors: _____   Size: _____

Markings: _____

Behavior

Sketch

Notes

Name: _____

Scientific Name: _____

Date: _____   Time: _____

Location: _____

Season

Winter   Spring

Summer   Fall

Weather

Temperature: _____

Habitat

Physical Description

Colors: _____   Size: _____

Markings: _____

Behavior

Sketch

Notes

Name: _____

Scientific Name: _____

Date: _____   Time: _____

Location: _____

Season	Weather
Winter Spring	
Summer Fall	Temperature: _____

Habitat

Physical Description

Colors: _____   Size: _____

Markings: _____

Behavior

Sketch

Notes

Name: _____

Scientific Name: _____

Date: _____   Time: _____

Location: _____

Season	Weather
Winter Spring Summer Fall	 Temperature: ____

Habitat

Physical Description

Colors: _____   Size: _____

Markings: _____

Behavior

Sketch

Notes

Name: _____

Scientific Name: _____

Date: _____   Time: _____

Location: _____

Season

Winter   Spring

Summer   Fall

Weather

Temperature: _____

Habitat

Physical Description

Colors: _____   Size: _____

Markings: _____

Behavior

Sketch

Notes

Name: _____

Scientific Name: _____

Date:_____   Time:_____

Location: _____

Season	Weather
Winter Spring	☀ ☁ 🌧 🌨 💨
Summer Fall	Temperature: _____

Habitat

Physical Description

Colors: _____   Size: _____

Markings:_____

Behavior

Sketch

Notes

Name: _____

Scientific Name: _____

Date: _____   Time: _____

Location: _____

Season	Weather
Winter Spring	
Summer Fall	Temperature: _____

Habitat

Physical Description

Colors: _____   Size: _____

Markings: _____

Behavior

Sketch

Notes

Name: _____

Scientific Name: _____

Date:_____   Time:_____

Location: _____

Season	Weather
Winter Spring	
Summer Fall	Temperature: _____

Habitat

Physical Description

Colors: _____   Size: _____

Markings:_____

Behavior

Sketch

Notes

Name: _____

Scientific Name: _____

Date:_____   Time:_____

Location: _____

Season	Weather
Winter Spring	
Summer Fall	Temperature: ____

Habitat

Physical Description

Colors: _____   Size: _____

Markings:_____

Behavior

Sketch

Notes

Name: _____

Scientific Name: _____

Date: _____   Time: _____

Location: _____

Season	Weather
Winter Spring	☀ ☁ 🌧 🌨 💨
Summer Fall	Temperature: ____

Habitat

Physical Description

Colors: _____   Size: _____

Markings: _____

Behavior

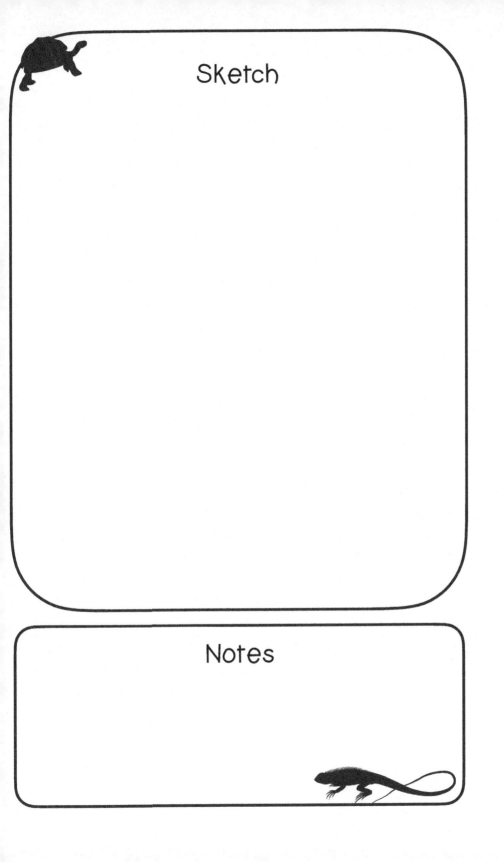

Sketch

Notes

Made in the USA
Las Vegas, NV
13 September 2023

77522181R00062